Published in Great Britain in MMXIII by
Book House, an imprint of
The Salariya Book Company Ltd
25 Marlborough Place, Brighton BN1 1UB
www.salariya.com
www.book-house.co.uk

PB ISBN-13: 978-1-908759-61-0

A CIP catalogue record for this book is available
from the British Library.
Printed and bound in China.
Printed on paper from sustainable sources.

Visit our website at **www.book-house.co.uk**
or go to **www.salariya.com**
for **free** electronic versions of:
You Wouldn't Want to be an Egyptian Mummy!
You Wouldn't Want to be a Roman Gladiator!
You Wouldn't Want to be a Polar Explorer!
You Wouldn't Want to Sail on a 19th-Century Whaling Ship!

Visit our **new** online shop at
shop.salariya.com
for great offers, gift ideas, all our new releases
and free postage and packaging.

BRIGHTON

A VERY PECULIAR HISTORY

QUIZ BOOK

With added
Hove, actually

CONTENTS

PUTTING BRIGHTON ON THE MAP

Q1

WHEN WERE THE BOROUGHS OF BRIGHTON AND HOVE OFFICIALLY MERGED?

a) 1995
b) 1996
c) 1997
d) 2000

Q2

WHAT DID ENGLISH WRITER WILLIAM HAZLITT DESCRIBE AS 'A COLLECTION OF STONE PUMPKINS AND PEPPER BOXES'?

a) Brighton Pier
b) Old Steine
c) The Royal Pavilion
d) Brighton Dome

LANES AND LAINES

THE LANES ARE THE LITTLE ALLEYWAYS IN THE OLDEST PART OF BRIGHTON – BORDERED BY NORTH STREET, EAST STREET, SHIP STREET AND THE TOWN HALL AREA. IN THE EARLY DAYS THIS WAS A HUMBLE FISHERMEN'S QUARTER CALLED HEMPSHARES, WHERE HEMP WAS EITHER GROWN OR TWISTED INTO ROPE. TODAY IT IS THE HOME OF JEWELLERS, ANTIQUE SHOPS AND OTHER FASHIONABLE OUTLETS.

LAINES WERE FIVE MEDIEVAL FIELDS ON THE DOWNLAND AROUND BRIGHTON: WEST LAINE, NORTH LAINE, HILLY LAINE, LITTLE LAINE AND EAST LAINE. THEY WERE DIVIDED INTO 'FURLONGS', SEPARATED FROM ONE ANOTHER BY PATHS KNOWN AS 'LEAKWAYS'. WHEN THE TOWN SPREAD OUTWARDS IN THE 18TH AND 19TH CENTURIES, THESE PATHS BECAME MAJOR EAST–WEST ROADS ACROSS THE TOWN, SUCH AS WESTERN ROAD AND ST JAMES'S STREET.

THE NORTH LAINE (BELOW THE RAILWAY STATION AND SEVERAL BLOCKS NORTH OF THE LANES) IS NOW AN EXCITING, OFFBEAT AREA PACKED WITH WACKY ONE-OFF SHOPS. DON'T MAKE THE MISTAKE OF CALLING THIS AREA THE 'NORTH LAINES' (PLURAL), OR YOU'LL SHOW EVERYONE THAT YOU'RE A 'FURRINER'!

Q3

WHAT WAS BRIGHTON CALLED IN THE DOMESDAY BOOK?

a) Bristelmestune
b) London-by-the-Sea
c) Hove
d) Brighthelmston

Q4

HOW MUCH WAS THE MANOR OF BRIGHTON VALUED AT IN THE DOMESDAY BOOK?

a) £5
b) £12
c) £33
d) £70

THANK YOUR LUCKY STONES

BEACH STONES WITH HOLES IN THEM ARE SOMETIMES FOUND ON BRIGHTON BEACH. THE PEOPLE OF SUSSEX USED TO WEAR THESE 'HAG STONES' ON STRINGS AROUND THEIR NECKS TO WARD OFF WITCHES AND OTHER EVILS, AND FISHERMEN WOULD NEVER GO TO SEA WITHOUT A COLLECTION OF THEM ON THEIR BOATS.

ONE TRADITION STILL REMEMBERED BY OLDER FOLK WAS TO SPIT THROUGH THE HOLE AND THEN THROW THE STONE OVER YOUR LEFT SHOULDER.

Q5

WHICH RIVER USED TO RUN DOWN THE COURSE OF THE PRESENT-DAY LONDON ROAD AND MEET THE SEA AT POOL VALLEY?

a) Ouse
b) Rother
c) Thames
d) Wellesbourne

Q6

WHAT REDUCED THE VILLAGE OF HANGLETON FROM A POPULATION OF 200 TO ONLY TWO HOUSEHOLDS BY 1428?

a) Terrible floods
b) Bubonic plague
c) A serial killer
d) A fire

Q7

WHICH OF THE FOLLOWING HAS THE PEPPER POT, JUST NORTH OF QUEEN'S PARK, NOT BEEN USED FOR?

a) A scout hut
b) An artist's studio
c) A printworks for the *Brighton Daily Mail*
d) A coffee shop

Q8

WHAT WAS COMPLETELY DESTROYED BY A TERRIBLE STORM IN 1896?

a) Henry Phillips's dome in Palmeira Square
b) The West Pier
c) The Royal Pavilion
d) The Chain Pier

BATHING MACHINES

THE BEACHES FOR MEN AND WOMEN WERE MIXED AT FIRST, BUT ATTITUDES CHANGED AND AFTER 1800 THEY WERE CAREFULLY SEGREGATED. HERE'S AN ADVERTISEMENT AIMED AT WOMEN:

'THIS IS TO ACQUAINT THE NOBILITY, GENTRY AND OTHERS RESORTING TO BRIGHTHELMSTON THAT MARTHA TUTT, MARY GUILDFORD, SUSANNAH GUILDFORD, ELIZABETH WINGHAM AND ANN SMITH, FIVE STRONG WOMEN, ALL USED TO THE SEA, HAVE COMPLETELY FITTED UP A SET OF NEW MACHINES, WITH A CAREFUL MAN AND A HORSE, TO CONDUCT THEM IN AND OUT OF THE WATER, FOR THE PURPOSE OF BATHING LADIES AND CHILDREN.'

Q9

WHAT WAS BRIGHTON PIER USED FOR BEFORE IT BECAME THE PALACE OF FUN AMUSEMENT ARCADE?

a) A discotheque
b) A fish restaurant
c) A zoo
d) A winter garden

Q10

WHEN DID THE DUKE OF YORK'S PICTURE HOUSE OPEN, MAKING IT THE OLDEST CONTINUOUSLY OPERATING CINEMA IN BRITAIN?

a) 1888
b) 1902
c) 1910
d) 1923

Q11

WHICH OF THE FOLLOWING FILMS WAS *NOT* SET IN
BRIGHTON?

a) *Quadrophenia*
b) *The Trials of Oscar Wilde*
c) *Brighton Rock*
d) *Summer Holiday*

Q12

HOW LONG DID IT TAKE TO TRAVEL FROM THE
STEINE TO THE STATION ON THE ELECTRIC
TRAMWAY?

a) 5 minutes
b) 8 minutes
c) 17 minutes
d) 30 minutes

Q13

WHERE WILL YOU FIND THE FOLLOWING WELCOME TO ALL WHO DRIVE INTO THE TOWN: 'HAIL GUEST, WE ASK NOT WHAT THOU ART. IF FRIEND WE GREET THEE HAND AND HEART. IF STRANGER SUCH NO LONGER BE. IF FOE OUR LOVE SHALL CONQUER THEE'?

a) Painted on the roadside of the A27
b) On a plaque on a large tree beside the A23
c) On one of the pylons on the A23
d) Nowhere

DID YOU KNOW?

THREE ARCHITECTS WERE RESPONSIBLE FOR MOST OF THE REGENCY ARCHITECTURE FOR WHICH BRIGHTON AND HOVE ARE FAMOUS: AMON WILDS, HIS SON AMON HENRY WILDS, AND THEIR PARTNER CHARLES AUGUSTIN BUSBY.

Q14

WHAT CAUSED THE BEACHES TO BE CLOSED TO THE PUBLIC IN 1940?

a) An oil slick
b) The Second World War
c) Only royalty were permitted on the beaches
d) High risk of shark attacks

Q15

WHAT IS AFFECTIONATELY KNOWN AS 'THE WEDDING CAKE'?

a) The concrete entrance to the Marina
b) Amex House
c) The Clock Tower
d) The Brighton Centre

Q16

IN WHICH YEAR WAS THE GRAND HOTEL DAMAGED BY AN IRA BOMB?

a) 1980
b) 1983
c) 1984
d) 1987

THE GRAND HOTEL BOMB

WHEN THE BOMB WENT OFF JUST BEFORE 3.00AM, THE HARD-WORKING PRIME MINISTER, MARGARET THATCHER, WAS STILL UP, PREPARING FOR THE FOLLOWING DAY'S BUSINESS. SHE SURVIVED — AND ADDRESSED THE CONSERVATIVE PARTY CONFERENCE THAT DAY AS PLANNED — BUT FIVE PEOPLE WERE KILLED AND ANOTHER 34 WERE INJURED.

Q17

WHERE DOES THE PLACE NAME WHITEHAWK ORIGINATE FROM?

a) It means 'valley of the hawks'.
b) It was the settlement of a man called Hawk.
c) It means 'yellow pond'.
d) Nobody knows.

Q18

WHO OPENED BRIGHTON MARINA IN 1979?

a) Margaret Thatcher
b) The Queen
c) Chris Eubank
d) Martha Gunn

19

Q19

WHERE CAN 'THE TOLMEN OR HOLY STONE OF THE DRUIDS' BE FOUND?

a) Hove Park
b) Queen's Park
c) Brighton Museum
d) Brighton Marina

Q20

ON WHICH STREET DID A MAN CALLED BULLOCK WIN A RUNNING RACE AGAINST RICHARD BARRYMORE, A DRINKING PAL OF THE PRINCE REGENT?

a) Ship Street
b) St James's Street
c) East Street
d) Black Lion Lane

MURDER IN THE BALCOMBE TUNNEL

ON THE AFTERNOON OF MONDAY 27 JUNE 1881, A YOUNG MAN NAMED PERCY LEFROY STAGGERED OFF AN EXPRESS TRAIN AT BRIGHTON, COVERED IN BLOOD.

HE TOLD STATION STAFF THAT HE HAD BEEN SHOT, BUT THE TRUTH WAS THAT LEFROY HIMSELF HAD JUST KILLED THE 64-YEAR-OLD COIN DEALER FREDERICK GOLD WHILE THE TRAIN WAS DEEP IN THE BALCOMBE TUNNEL. THIS 'RAILWAY MURDER' BECAME NOTORIOUS; THE *DAILY TELEGRAPH* CALLED IT 'ONE OF THE MOST ASTONISHINGLY CRUEL AND COLD-BLOODED ASSASSINATIONS OF MODERN TIMES.'

BECAUSE OF BUNGLING BY A DETECTIVE CALLED HOLMES (QUITE CLEARLY NOT SHERLOCK), LEFROY MANAGED TO ESCAPE, BUT HE WAS EVENTUALLY CAPTURED AND BROUGHT TO TRIAL.

A VAIN MAN, LEFROY ASKED PERMISSION TO WEAR FULL EVENING DRESS IN COURT, BECAUSE HE THOUGHT THIS WOULD IMPRESS THE JURY. THIS REQUEST WAS REFUSED, ALTHOUGH HE WAS ALLOWED TO CARRY HIS SILK HAT — AND APPEARED TO TAKE MORE INTEREST IN IT THAN HE DID IN THE COURT PROCEEDINGS.

HE WAS HANGED AT LEWES.

THE LOCALS

Q21

WHOSE SHIN-BONE WAS DISCOVERED WHILE ARCHAEOLOGISTS WERE EXPLORING AN ANCIENT RAISED BEACH AT BOXGROVE, 32 KM WEST OF BRIGHTON?

a) Ted's
b) Roger's
c) Simon's
d) The Prince Regent's

Q22

ACCORDING TO THE LEGEND OF DEVIL'S DYKE, WHO HAD A CUNNING PLAN TO DROWN ALL THE LITTLE CHURCHES OF THE SUSSEX DOWNS IN A SINGLE NIGHT BY DIGGING A VAST TRENCH?

a) Roger
b) The Long Man of Wilmington
c) The Celts
d) Old Scratch

BRIGHTON FESTIVAL

EVERY MAY THE TOWN IS CRAMMED WITH PEOPLE ATTENDING PLAYS, CONCERTS, READINGS, EXHIBITIONS AND STREET EVENTS. IT'S THE BIGGEST ARTS FESTIVAL IN ENGLAND — AND IT'S STILL GROWING.

Q23

AS DERRICK CARVER, A FLEMISH BREWER WHO HAD SET UP HIS BUSINESS IN BLACK LION STREET, WAS BEING BURNT AT THE STAKE FOR BEING PROTESTANT IN BLOODY MARY'S REIGN, WHAT DID HE THROW INTO THE CROWD?

a) His bible
b) His mobile phone
c) His hat
d) His shoes

Q24

WHOSE MEMORIAL IN ST NICHOLAS'S CHURCHYARD
INCLUDES THE LINES: 'WHEN CHARLES YE GREATE
WAS NOTHING BUT A BREATH, THIS VALIANT SOULE
STEPT BETWEEN HIM AND DEATH'?

a) Colonel George Gounter
b) Lord Wilmot
c) Nicholas Tettersell
d) King Arthur

THERE'S PLENTY OF DIPPERS AND JOKERS
AND SALT-WATER RIGS FOR YOUR FUN;
THE KING OF THEM ALL IS OLD SMOAKER,
THE QUEEN OF THEM ALL, MARTHA GUNN.

Q25

WHAT WAS 'THE FASHION'?

a) A way of wearing one's hat, inspired by local fishermen
b) Wealthy people who flocked to Brighton from Lewes, Tunbridge Wells and London
c) A group of artists who pioneered a radical new sculpting technique using clay
d) An exciting, off-beat area packed with wacky one-off shops

Q26

WHO WAS MARTHA GUNN?

a) A famous librarian
b) The landlady of a famous public house
c) A famous 'dipper'
d) A famous 'dripper'

Q27

WHO WAS 'PRINNY'?

a) King George IV
b) Prince Regent
c) George Augustus Frederick, Prince of Wales
d) All of the above

A DAY AT THE RACES

PART OF THE DUKE OF CUMBERLAND'S 'ROISTERING' (AN EXPRESSIVE OLD WORD) INVOLVED TRAVELLING TO LEWES FOR THE RACES, AND AFTER A WHILE HE AND HIS FRIENDS HAD THE BRIGHT IDEA OF SETTING UP A RACECOURSE OF THEIR OWN ON THE DOWNS ABOVE BRIGHTON — THE VERY ONE WE KNOW TODAY.

Q28

WHAT IS THE WAIST MEASUREMENT OF THE PRINCE REGENT'S BREECHES, NOW IN BRIGHTON MUSEUM?

a) 24 inches
b) 34 inches
c) 42 inches
d) 50 inches

Q29

WHO WAS THE PRINCE REGENT'S SECOND WIFE, DESCRIBED AS A WOMAN 'OF INDELICATE MANNERS, INDIFFERENT CHARACTER AND NOT VERY INVITING APPEARANCE'?

a) Caroline of Brunswick
b) Maria Fitzherbert
c) Martha Gunn
d) Anne of Cleves

Q30

WHAT HAPPENED TO HENRY PHILLIPS WHEN HIS 'TROPICAL WONDERLAND,' THE ANTHAEUM, IN PALMEIRA SQUARE CRASHED TO THE GROUND IN A HEAP OF GLASS AND MANGLED IRON?

a) He went blind.
b) He had a heart attack.
c) He went deaf.
d) He ran away and was never seen again.

DID YOU KNOW?

AN 18TH-CENTURY HOUSE OFF DUKE STREET, IN THE OLD TOWN, HAS WALLS COVERED IN WOOD BLOCKS TO IMITATE STONE. IT STANDS IN A WALLED YARD SET BACK FROM THE STREET.

Q31

THE PRINCE REGENT'S BROTHER, WILLIAM IV, WAS PRONE TO SOME RATHER ECCENTRIC BEHAVIOUR, BUT WHAT DID HE HAVE A TERRIBLE HABIT OF DOING IN PUBLIC?

a) Spitting
b) Swearing
c) Picking his nose
d) Tap dancing

Q32

WHO SOLD THE ROYAL PAVILION TO THE LOCAL COUNCIL IN 1850?

a) King William IV
b) Queen Victoria
c) Prinny
d) The White Lady

Q33

FRED GINNETT, A VICTORIAN CIRCUS PROPRIETOR,
IS BURIED IN WOODVALE CEMETERY, BUT WHAT
STATUE SITS ON TOP OF HIS TOMB?

a) A bowing circus horse
b) A trapeze artist
c) A circus elephant
d) A prowling circus tiger

Q34

WHICH QUEEN IS QUEEN'S PARK NAMED AFTER?

a) Queen Victoria
b) Queen Boudicca
c) Queen Adelaide
d) The band Queen

Q35

IN 1903 HOW DID THE AMERICAN MUSIC-HALL ARTISTE 'MISS FLORENCE' TRAVEL FROM LONDON TO BRIGHTON?

a) Walked on a ball
b) Rode standing on horseback
c) Roller-skated
d) Rode a unicycle

ALTERNATIVE BRIGHTON

KEMP TOWN IN PARTICULAR HAS LONG BEEN A MAGNET FOR THE GAY COMMUNITY — WHICH IN BRIGHTON, AT LEAST, IS NO LONGER REGARDED AS BEING ON THE FRINGE AT ALL — AND THERE ARE PUBS, CLUBS AND 'PINK PARLOURS' GALORE.

IT'S JUST NOT CRICKET

THE SUSSEX COUNTY CRICKET CLUB WAS FOUNDED IN 1839, BUT HAD TO WAIT UNTIL 2003 TO WIN THE CHAMPIONSHIP FOR THE VERY FIRST TIME - AND THEN WON IT IN 2006 AND 2007, TOO.

Q36

C. B. FRY WAS PROBABLY THE GREATEST SPORTING ALL-ROUNDER EVER, BUT WHICH OF THESE STATEMENTS IS *NOT* TRUE?

a) He captained Oxford University at Cricket.
b) He played in an FA Cup final.
c) He held the world long-jump record.
d) He won a silver medal at the Olympics.

Q37

WHO PERFORMED AT THE BRIGHTON CENTRE IN
1977 IN WHAT TURNED OUT TO BE THE LAST
PERFORMANCE OF HIS LIFE?

a) Bob Hope
b) Louis Armstrong
c) Frank Sinatra
d) Bing Crosby

Q38

WHAT HAPPENED TO THE BRONZE STATUE OF STEVE
OVETT, WORLD RECORD HOLDER AND OLYMPIC
GOLD MEDALLIST, IN PRESTON PARK?

a) It was stolen, leaving only his feet.
b) It melted.
c) The head was stolen.
d) It had such a poor likeness to Steve Ovett
   that he requested it be taken down.

TEN NOVELS SET* IN BRIGHTON

1. *PRIDE AND PREJUDICE* (JANE AUSTEN, 1813)

2. *DOMBEY AND SON* (CHARLES DICKENS, 1848)

3. *THE NEWCOMES* (WILLIAM MAKEPEACE THACKERAY, 1855)

4. *OVINGDEAN GRANGE* (WILLIAM HARRISON AINSWORTH, 1860)

5. *NEW GRUB STREET* (GEORGE GISSING, 1891)

6. *HILDA LESSWAYS* (ARNOLD BENNETT, 1911)

7. *BRIGHTON ROCK* (GRAHAM GREENE, 1938)

8. *HANGOVER SQUARE* (PATRICK HAMILTON, 1941)

9. *SUGAR RUSH* (JULIE BURCHILL, 2004)

10. *DEAD SIMPLE* (PETER JAMES, 2005)

* AT LEAST IN PART

Q39

THE PRINCE REGENTS' FIRST (UNOFFICIAL) WIFE WAS MARIA FITZHERBERT. WHAT WAS THE NAME OF HER FIRST HUSBAND WHO, WITHIN A YEAR OF MARRIAGE, TOPPLED FROM HIS HORSE AND DIED?

a) George IV
b) Edward Weld
c) Thomas Fitzherbert
d) Duke of Cumberland

Q40

WHO INTRODUCED THE FIRST TELEPHONE SERVICE TO BRIGHTON?

a) Henry Phillips
b) Queen Victoria
c) Magnus Volk
d) Alexander Phones

WORK AND PLAY

Q41

A CUP FASHIONED FROM A SINGLE PIECE OF RED AMBER WAS FOUND IN AN OAK COFFIN SOME 3 METRES BELOW THE SURFACE AND IS NOW DISPLAYED IN HOVE MUSEUM, BUT WHICH AGE IS IT FROM?

a) The Bronze Age
b) The Iron Age
c) The Stone Age
d) The Metal Age

Q42

WHICH OF THE FOLLOWING DID ARCHAEOLOGISTS *NOT* FIND IN OR AROUND THE VILLA DISCOVERED IN 1876 CLOSE TO PRESTON PARK?

a) Bronze tweezers
b) A pin made of bone
c) An iron lamp
d) A glass vase

Q43

ACCORDING TO THE DOMESDAY BOOK, ALDRINGTON HAD 51 VILLAGERS AND 22 SMALLHOLDERS BUT ONLY ONE WHAT?

a) Hall
b) Pig
c) Slave
d) Tree

ANYONE WHO DOES NOT LIVE IN BRIGHTON MUST BE MAD AND OUGHT TO BE LOCKED UP.

S. P. B. MAIS

Q44

WHAT ARE 'TWITTENS'?

a) A name for local fishermen
b) Stallholders at Brighton's market
c) A type of chimney
d) The little alleyways in the oldest part of Brighton

DID YOU KNOW?

BY 1650, WHILE HOVE WAS STILL LITTLE MORE THAN A ROW OF COTTAGES IN HOVE STREET, BRIGHTON HAD BECOME THE LARGEST TOWN IN SUSSEX, WITH A POPULATION OF AROUND 4,000.

CO-OPERATIVE FISHERMEN

A 'BOOK OF ANCIENT CUSTOMS' RECORDS THAT IN 1580 THERE WERE 400 FISHERMEN IN BRIGHTON, WITH 80 BOATS AND 10,000 NETS. THEY WORKED AS A CO-OPERATIVE: ALL HAD SHARES IN THE CATCH, WITH A PERCENTAGE ALSO GOING TOWARDS THE TOWN'S DEFENCES AND THE MAINTENANCE OF THE CHURCH.

Q45

WHAT IS THE NAME OF A SHALLOW BOAT DEVELOPED BY LOCAL FISHERMAN THAT WAS BROAD IN THE BEAM, HAD TRIANGULAR LEE-BOARDS AND WAS DESCRIBED AS 'A SMALL, ROUND LITTLE TUB'?

a) A Brighton Hoggie
b) A Brighton Jug
c) A Brighton Soggie
d) A Brighton Tub-Boat

Q46

WHICH OF THESE CONDITIONS COULD SUPPOSEDLY BE CURED BY BRIGHTON'S 'SEA WATER CURE', AS PROPOSED BY DR RICHARD RUSSELL, A LEWES MEDICAL MAN?

a) Poor hearing
b) Bad breath
c) Head lice
d) Yellow teeth

SEA WATER CURE

RUSSELL WASN'T THE FIRST PERSON TO THINK THE SEASIDE WAS HEALTHY — PEOPLE WERE ALREADY COMING TO BRIGHTON — BUT IN 1750 HE PUBLISHED A BOOK WITH THE CATCHY TITLE *A DISSERTATION ON THE USE OF SEAWATER IN THE DISEASES OF THE GLANDS*. IN CASE THAT SOUNDED TOO EXCITING, HE WROTE IT IN LATIN, BUT THREE YEARS LATER HE BROUGHT OUT AN ENGLISH VERSION AND EVERYONE BEGAN TO TAKE NOTICE OF HIM.

IN THE ROYAL PAVILION

THE FANTASTIC CENTRAL CHANDELIER (OR GASOLIER) IN THE BANQUETING ROOM IS 9 METRES (30 FEET) HIGH AND WEIGHS ONE TONNE. IT WAS ORIGINALLY LIT BY NEWFANGLED GAS. THERE ARE FOUR SMALLER CHANDELIERS DECORATED WITH LOTUS-LEAF DESIGNS.

Q47

THE PRINCE REGENT BUILT THE BRIGHTON DOME, CONNECTED BY AN UNDERGROUND TUNNEL TO HIS ROYAL PAVILION, BUT WHAT WAS THE DOME'S ORIGINAL PURPOSE?

a) A theatre
b) A banqueting room
c) Stables and indoor riding school
d) A school

Q48

WHAT ARE THE STAIRS AND BALUSTRADES RISING FROM THE GROUND FLOOR IN THE ROYAL PAVILION MADE FROM?

a) Iron
b) Bamboo
c) Wood
d) Plastic

Q49

AFTER THE ROYAL PAVILION WAS FINISHED, HOW MANY TIMES DID THE PRINCE REGENT VISIT IT BEFORE HE DIED IN 1830?

a) None
b) 1
c) 3
d) 20

SHE WENT FOR A SOLDIER

PHOEBE HESSEL (1713–1821) DISGUISED HERSELF AS A MAN AND ENLISTED AS A SOLDIER IN ORDER TO FOLLOW HER SWEETHEART ALL OVER EUROPE.

HER GRAVESTONE IN ST NICHOLAS'S CHURCHYARD TELLS US THAT SHE SERVED FOR MANY YEARS IN THE 5TH REGIMENT OF FOOT, WAS WOUNDED BY A BAYONET IN THE BATTLE OF FONTENOY (1745) AND SURVIVED UNTIL THE GRAND OLD AGE OF 108.

HER LONG LIFE, WE READ, 'COMMENCED IN THE TIME OF QUEEN ANNE AND EXTENDED TO THE REIGN OF GEORGE IV, BY WHOSE MUNIFICENCE SHE RECEIVED COMFORT AND SUPPORT IN HER LATTER YEARS'.

THERE'S A SUGGESTION THAT PHOEBE INVENTED SOME OF THE COLOURFUL DETAILS ABOUT HER LIFE — BUT PRINNY ALWAYS ENJOYED A CHARACTER (BEING AN OUTSIZED ONE HIMSELF) AND HE GRANTED HER A PENSION OF HALF A GUINEA (52½P) A YEAR FOR LIFE.

Q50

WHAT ARE 'MATHEMATICAL TILES'?

a) Circular floor tiles.
b) Clay tiles shaped to look like bricks.
c) Tiles used in schools to help teach children algebra.
d) Bathroom tiles shaped like shells.

PITY THE POOR HORSES

IN THE HEYDAY OF THE STAGECOACHES (OR 'FLYING MACHINES'), DIFFERENT COMPANIES COMPETED WITH EACH OTHER TO CARRY THEIR PASSENGERS FASTEST BETWEEN LONDON AND BRIGHTON. THIS WAS BAD NEWS FOR THE EXHAUSTED HORSES WHICH HAD TO PULL THEM NON-STOP. IN A SINGLE WEEK IN 1816, NO FEWER THAN 15 HORSES DIED – AND AFTER THIS NEW RULES WERE BROUGHT IN TO PROTECT THEM.

KILLED BY A TRAM

BRIGHTON'S TRAMS HAD AN EXCELLENT SAFETY RECORD OVERALL, BUT AT 7 O' CLOCK ON A BLUSTERY DECEMBER MORNING IN 1935 THE BRAKES FAILED ON A NO. 74 AS IT RAN ALONG THE STEEP PART OF DITCHLING ROAD NORTH OF THE LEVEL. IT JUMPED THE POINTS AT UNION ROAD AND OVERTURNED. TWENTY-FOUR PEOPLE WERE INJURED, AND A CYCLIST HIT BY THE TRAM WAS KILLED.

PHONE BOXES

THERE AREN'T MANY OF THE OLD-STYLE RED TELEPHONE BOXES LEFT FROM THE 1930S, BUT LOOK OUT FOR THEM IN DYKE ROAD (NEAR ST NICHOLAS'S CHURCH), NEW ROAD, PELHAM SQUARE, POWIS SQUARE, ST PETER'S PLACE AND UPPER NORTH STREET.

Q51

WHO WERE THE BRIGHTON TIGERS?

a) An ice hockey club
b) A swimming club
c) A chess club
d) A group of artists

Q52

WHERE DID THE FIRST TRAIN TO STEAM INTO BRIGHTON STATION IN 1841 COME FROM?

a) London Victoria
b) Clapham Junction
c) London Bridge
d) Hove

Q53

WHAT WAS THE NAME OF THE ELECTRIC CONTRAPTION WHICH CARRIED PASSENGERS ON STILTS HIGH ABOVE THE WAVES AS IT RAN TO ROTTINGDEAN ON UNDERWATER RAILS?

a) The Octopus
b) The Daddy-Long-Legs
c) The Spider
d) The Snail

BUILT TO LAST?

THE ARCHITECTURAL WRITER SIR NIKOLAUS PEVSNER DESCRIBED HOVE'S VICTORIAN TOWN HALL AS 'SO RED, SO GOTHIC, SO HARD, SO IMPERISHABLE'. UNFORTUNATELY, ON 9 JANUARY 1966 – ONLY A FEW WEEKS AFTER HE HAD WRITTEN THOSE WORDS – THE BUILDING WENT UP IN FLAMES.

Q54

WHAT ENTERTAINED THE CROWDS TWICE A DAY AT THE BRIGHTON AQUARIUM, NOW CALLED THE SEA LIFE CENTRE?

a) Octopus feeding time
b) Organ recitals
c) Poetry readings
d) A clown

THE SEAGULLS

BRIGHTON AND HOVE ALBION, ALIAS 'THE SEAGULLS', PLAYED IN THE TOP DIVISION OF THE FOOTBALL LEAGUE (NOW THE PREMIERSHIP) FROM 1979 UNTIL THEY WERE RELEGATED IN 1983 – THE YEAR IN WHICH THEY REACHED THE CUP FINAL AGAINST MANCHESTER UNITED, NARROWLY MISSED A LAST-MINUTE WINNER AND THEN LOST 4-0 IN THE REPLAY.

Q55

WHY DID PEOPLE SOON PUT A STOP TO MAGNUS VOLK'S 'TIME BALL' ON THE TOP OF BRIGHTON'S CLOCK TOWER?

a) It was too noisy as it moved up and down its mast every hour.
b) It told inaccurate time.
c) It was under constant attack from seagulls.
d) It fell off and injured a passer-by.

Q56

ON 17 JUNE 1934, WHAT WAS FOUND IN A FOUL-SMELLING TRUNK AT THE LEFT-LUGGAGE OFFICE OF BRIGHTON RAILWAY STATION?

a) Lots of stinky cheese
b) The torso of a young woman
c) Rotting meat
d) Dirty laundry

Q57

WHAT HAPPENED TO THE FAMILIES WATCHING THE FILM *THE GHOST COMES HOME* IN THE ODEON CINEMA ON 14 SEPTEMBER 1940?

a) A bomb was dropped on the cinema.
b) They all saw a ghost.
c) The cinema started leaking.
d) The popcorn was poisoned.

Q58

HOW MANY STUDENTS ENROLLED AT SUSSEX UNIVERSITY WHEN IT OPENED IN OCTOBER 1961?

a) 23
b) 52
c) 169
d) 4,988

Q59

WHY DID LORD OLIVIER JOIN A PROTEST AGAINST
BRITISH RAIL IN 1970?

a) British Rail withdrew the luxurious Brighton
Belle from service.
b) Ticket prices for the Brighton Belle became
too expensive.
c) British Rail decided to take kippers off the
breakfast menu on the Brighton Belle.
d) British Rail wanted to change the name of
the train from Brighton Belle to Brighton
Beau.

THE FIRST AMATEUR LONDON TO BRIGHTON RUNNING EVENT
WAS A GO-AS-YOU-PLEASE CONTEST ORGANISED BY SOUTH
LONDON HARRIERS IN 1899. THE WINNER, F. D. RANDALL OF
FINCHLEY HARRIERS, RAN THE DISTANCE IN 6 HOURS, 58
MINUTES, 18 SECONDS. ON THE STRENGTH OF THIS RUN, THE
FIRST THREE MEN HOME WERE SELECTED TO COMPETE FOR
GREAT BRITAIN IN THE 1900 OLYMPIC MARATHON.

Q60

WHICH FILM WAS INSPIRED BY BRIGHTON'S BANK HOLIDAY RIOTS IN 1964?

a) *Quadrophenia*
b) *Jigsaw*
c) *Bank Holiday*
d) *Oh! What a Lovely War*

A VISIT TO BRIGHTON COMPRISED EVERY POSSIBILITY OF EARTHLY HAPPINESS.

JANE AUSTEN,
PRIDE AND PREJUDICE

Q61

THE AREA AROUND KENSINGTON GARDENS IS CALLED THE NORTH LAINE, BUT WHAT IS A LAINE?

a) An area designed purely for shopping
b) A narrow road
c) A medieval field
d) A type of tree

Q62

WHICH BRIGHTON-AREA PLACE NAME MEANS 'YELLOW POND' IN OLD ENGLISH?

a) Falmer
b) Ovingdean
c) Stanmer
d) Bevendean

Q63

WHAT DID SMART BUSINESSMEN BOTTLE AND SELL IN LONDON AS 'OCEANIC FLUID?'

a) Scarborough sea water
b) Brighton sea water
c) River water
d) Beer

Q64

WHICH POET AND ESSAYIST REFERRED TO THE BRIGHTON 'DIPPERS' AS 'LIMBS OF SATAN'?

a) Edward Calf
b) Trevor Veal
c) Charles Lamb
d) Jonathan Foal

Q65

WHAT WAS THE HINDOOSTANEE COFFEE HOUSE, OPENED IN LONDON IN 1810?

a) An Indian takeaway
b) A coffee shop
c) A yoga centre
d) A bookshop

BURNING THE CLOCKS

BRIGHTON HAS ITS OWN FIRE FESTIVAL ON 21 DECEMBER TO MARK THE WINTER SOLSTICE. THERE'S A PARADE WITH BANDS AND SPECTACULAR HOMEMADE LANTERNS (WHICH, LIKE SO MANY BRIGHTON EVENTS, ENDS IN MADEIRA DRIVE), AFTER WHICH THE LANTERNS ARE BURNT ON BRIGHTON BEACH AND A GRAND FIREWORKS DISPLAY LIGHTS UP THE SKY OVER THE ENGLISH CHANNEL.

Q66

WHY DID PHOEBE HESSEL (1713–1821) DISGUISE HERSELF AS A MAN AND ENLIST AS A SOLDIER?

a) To be close to her twin brother
b) To follow her sweetheart all over Europe
c) To run away from the circus
d) To visit Paris

Q67

WHAT IS THE LARGEST CRESCENT IN BRITAIN?

a) Royal Crescent
b) Grosvenor Square
c) Sussex Square
d) Brighton Crescent

Q68

WHICH OF THE FOLLOWING IS ONE OF THE MANY GHOSTS THAT ARE SAID TO HAUNT PRESTON MANOR?

a) Prinny
b) The Woman in Black
c) The Town Hall Cat
d) The White Lady

Q69

IN 1889, HOW MANY BEER-HOUSES OF DIFFERENT KINDS WERE THERE REPORTEDLY IN BRIGHTON?

a) 209
b) 452
c) 653
d) 774

THE BEACH

IT'S THE BEACH WHICH GIVES BRIGHTON ITS EDGE. IT'S BEEN SMARTENED UP OVER THE PAST FEW YEARS, AND THERE'S PLENTY TO DO AND SEE IN THE VICINITY:

- THE PIER (IT'S FREE TO ENTER)
- NIGHTCLUBS (MAINLY ON THE SEAFRONT AND IN WEST STREET)
- OPEN-AIR CONCERTS BY FATBOY SLIM AND OTHERS
- BRIGHTON FISHING MUSEUM (UNDER THE ARCHES – ALSO FREE)
- ABSTRACT BEACH SCULPTURES
- SWIMMING (BUT DO WEAR BEACH SHOES)

Q70

WHICH OF THE FOLLOWING PLACES OF WORSHIP WAS BUILT AS A MISSION CHURCH FOR BRIGHTON'S FISHERMEN IN 1848?

a) All Saints
b) St Andrew
c) Chapel Royal
d) St Paul

Q71

WHICH ONE OF THESE NOVELS WAS NOT SET (AT LEAST IN PART) IN BRIGHTON?

a) *Brighton Rock*
b) *Sugar Rush*
c) *Dead Simple*
d) *Hard Times*

Q72

WHERE DID RUDYARD KIPLING LIVE UNTIL GAWPING TOURISTS DRIVE HIM AWAY TO BURWASH?

a) Bevendean
b) Rottingdean
c) Withdean
d) Whitehawk

THE NAMES ON THE BUSES

BRIGHTON AND HOVE'S DOUBLE-DECKER BUSES CARRY THE NAMES OF MANY PEOPLE WITH LOCAL CONNECTIONS. HERE ARE SOME OF THEM:

ENID BAGNOLD. THE AUTHOR OF *NATIONAL VELVET* LIVED FOR MORE THAN 50 YEARS AT NORTH END HOUSE IN ROTTINGDEAN.

OLIVER BULLEID. HE WAS ONE OF THE LEADING INNOVATORS IN LOCOMOTIVE DESIGN AND IS REMEMBERED BY RAILWAY ENTHUSIASTS FOR HIS WORK AS MECHANICAL ENGINEER TO THE OLD SOUTHERN RAILWAY.

ELLEN NYE CHART. TAKING OVER THE THEATRE ROYAL, AFTER HER HUSBAND'S DEATH IN 1875, SHE LAUNCHED A PERIOD OF REMARKABLE BRILLIANCE, ATTRACTING ACTORS SUCH AS SIR HENRY IRVING AND DAME ELLEN TERRY. HER GHOST IS SAID TO HAUNT THE THEATRE.

SIR WINSTON CHURCHILL. THE GREAT WAR LEADER ATTENDED A SCHOOL IN BRUNSWICK ROAD, HOVE, WHERE A FELLOW PUPIL STABBED HIM (NOT TOO SERIOUSLY) WITH A PENKNIFE.

SIR ROWLAND HILL. THE MAN WHO INVENTED THE PENNY POST, WHILE SECRETARY TO THE POST OFFICE IN THE 1850S, LIVED AT HANOVER CRESCENT. HE WAS ALSO A DIRECTOR OF THE LONDON, BRIGHTON & SOUTH COAST RAILWAY.

DOROTHY STRINGER. A COUNCILLOR, ALDERMAN AND MAYOR OF BRIGHTON, SHE SERVED FOR ALL OF 50 YEARS ON THE EDUCATION COMMITTEE WITHOUT MISSING A MEETING. A SCHOOL IS NAMED AFTER HER.

SIR CHARLES THOMAS-STANFORD. THE OWNER OF PRESTON MANOR, HE LEFT IT TO BRIGHTON COROPORATION ON HIS DEATH IN 1932.

BRIGHTON LOOKS LIKE A TOWN THAT IS CONSTANTLY HELPING THE POLICE WITH THEIR ENQUIRIES.

KEITH WATERHOUSE

ANSWERS

PUTTING BRIGHTON ON THE MAP

Q1: C. 1997

The Peace Statue on the seafront marks the dividing line between 'noisy, boisterous' Brighton and 'dull, unimaginative' Hove and local inhabitants are acutely aware of which side they live on.

Q2: C. THE ROYAL PAVILION

It is built in the Indo-Saracenic style prevalent in India for most of the 19th century, with the most extravagant chinoiserie interiors ever executed in the British Isles.

Q3: A. BRISTELMESTUNE

Before being called Brighton it was known as something like Brighthelmston, although more than 40 variations on the theme have been recorded.

Q4: B. £12

The locals had to pay Ralph, the tenant according to the Domesday Book, an annual rent of 4,000 herrings.

Q5: D. WELLESBOURNE

It was never much more than a stream for most of the year, but it became a bit more impressive at times of high rainfall and sometimes caused serious flooding around where it met the sea.

Q6: B. BUBONIC PLAGUE

In the 1540s, Richard Bellingham used stone from Lewes Priory (dismantled on the orders of Henry VIII) to build Hangleton Manor, which is now the oldest domestic building in all of Brighton and Hove.

Q7: D. A COFFEE SHOP

The Pepper Pot was part of a large villa built for Thomas Attree in 1830. Its architect was Charles Barry, who designed the Houses of Parliament (as well as St Peter's church in Brighton).

Q8: D. THE CHAIN PIER

The main purpose of the pier was to allow passengers to get on and off steamships without having to be ferried to the beach in rowing boats, but very soon 'the Fashion' discovered how pleasant it was to promenade along the decking, and a new entertainment was born.

Q9: D. A WINTER GARDEN

The Palace Pier is the second most visited 'leisure facility' in the whole of England and attracts 4.5 million visitors every year.

Q10: C. 1910

On the roof of the Duke of York's is a sculpture of a gigantic pair of high-kicking legs in striped stockings, which originally adorned an independent cinema in Oxford called the Moulin Rouge.

Q11: D. *SUMMER HOLIDAY*

Summer Holiday is set in a double-decker bus en route to the South of France. However, its eventual destination is Athens.

Q12: B. 8 MINUTES

Brighton's electric tramway system was launched in 1901, and within a few years there were 50 cars – several illuminated by coloured bulbs – travelling on just under 16km (10 miles) of track.

Q13: C. ON A PYLON ON THE A23

The pylons were unveiled by the Duke and Duchess of York (later George VI and Queen Elizabeth) in 1928.

Q14: B. THE SECOND WORLD WAR

In Brighton's heaviest air raid, on 25 May 1943, the town was dive-bombed by enemy fighters which strafed pedestrians in the street. 24 people were killed and 51 seriously injured.

Q15: B. AMEX HOUSE

Some 2,000 people work in the American Express European headquarters on Edward Street.

Q16: C. 1984

The hotel was later renovated and extended and Mrs Thatcher officially reopened it in August 1986.

Q17: D. NOBODY KNOWS

Moulsecoomb is so named because the man who ran the show in this 'coombe', or valley, was perhaps an obstinate character – 'Mul' was a nickname meaning 'mule'.

Q18: B. THE QUEEN

Covering a total of 51 hectares (126 acres), the marina complex contains 1,600 berths and 863 houses.

Q19: A. HOVE PARK

It originally lay on farmland at Goldstone Bottom, but in Victorian times the farmer got so fed up with sightseers trampling his crops that he sank a large hole and buried it.

Q20: D. BLACK LION LANE

Look out for the street yourself and you'll see why there was no way that Barrymore could have overtaken the portly Bullock.

THE MURDER OF A POLICE CHIEF

THE FIRST CHIEF CONSTABLE OF BRIGHTON WAS HENRY SOLOMON, AND BY 13 MARCH 1844 HE HAD BEEN IN THE POST FOR A LITTLE MORE THAN FIVE YEARS.

ON THAT EVENING A 23-YEAR-OLD MAN SUSPECTED OF STEALING WAS BROUGHT INTO THE POLICE STATION AT THE TOWN HALL. JOHN LAWRENCE WAS UNEMPLOYED AND A BIT OF A LAYABOUT, BUT HE HADN'T BEEN IN SERIOUS TROUBLE WITH THE POLICE BEFORE.

SOLOMON BRIEFLY QUESTIONED HIM AND, AS LAWRENCE APPEARED AGITATED, TOLD HIM TO SIT DOWN. SOME MINUTES LATER LAWRENCE SUDDENLY LEAPT TO HIS FEET, GRABBED A POKER FROM THE FIREPLACE, AND BROUGHT IT DOWN SAVAGELY ON SOLOMON'S HEAD. HE DIED FROM HIS INJURIES THE FOLLOWING MORNING.

LAWRENCE, FOUND GUILTY OF MURDER, WAS THE LAST PERSON TO BE HANGED IN PUBLIC AT HORSHAM GAOL.

THE LOCALS

Q21: B. ROGER'S

At least, that's what the archaeologists decided to call him. They also found a couple of teeth, but these probably belonged to someone else.

Q22: D. OLD SCRATCH

Apparently his frantic digging woke up a little old woman, who quickly saw what he was about. She set a candle in her window and put a sieve in front of it to create a glowing globe. When Old Scratch saw it, he thought it must be the rising sun and, unable to work after sunrise, he had to give up then and there.

Q23: A. HIS BIBLE

At his trial he told the bishop defiantly: 'You say that you can make a God. Ye can make a pudding as well.'

Q24: C. NICHOLAS TETTERSELL

Tettersell helped the future Charles II escape across the Channel at the end of the Civil War. He was so well rewarded at the Restoration that he was able to buy the Old Ship Inn on the seafront.

Q25: B. WEALTHY PEOPLE FROM OUTSIDE BRIGHTON

The broad, flat thoroughfare which runs past the Royal Pavilion to the sea was a fashionable promenade in Regency times. It's now called the Old Steine, and its name means 'stony place' in Old English.

Q26: C. A FAMOUS DIPPER

A dipper was a person who helped bathers out of their bathing machines and thrust them into the water.

Q27: D. ALL OF THE ABOVE

A terrible spendthrift, Prinny ran up huge debts and was a patron of new forms of leisure, style and taste.

Q28: D. 50 INCHES (127 CM)

The Prince Regent's cook was an eccentric German named Louis Weltje. Some said that he and his wife, could speak English no better than a pair of elephants.

Q29: A. CAROLINE OF BRUNSWICK

George thought that Caroline talked too much and was smelly, and so he turned up drunk to the wedding. As far as Caroline was concerned, the Prince was 'very fat and nothing like as handsome as his portrait'.

Q30: A. HE WENT BLIND

Some people say that, in a drought, you can still see the outlines of the Anthaeum in the parched grass.

Q31: A. SPITTING

Having served in the Royal Navy, he became known as the 'Sailor King'. At one New Year's Eve ball he took to the dance floor partnered by a 61-year-old admiral.

Q32: B. QUEEN VICTORIA

She decided that Osborne House on the Isle of Wight was a more pleasant place to stay.

Q33: A. A BOWING CIRCUS HORSE

Sir George Everest is buried in the churchyard of St Andrew's in Church Road, Hove. He is the former surveyor-general of India who gave his name to the highest mountain in the world.

Q34: C. QUEEN ADELAIDE

Adelaide Crescent in Hove is also named after Queen Adelaide, the wife of William IV.

Q35: A. WALKED ON A BALL

It took her five days!

Q36: D. SILVER MEDAL AT THE OLYMPICS

He wrote several books and stood as a Liberal candidate at elections in Brighton. He also claimed to have once turned down the throne of Albania!

Q37: D. BING CROSBY

The Brighton Centre opened on the seafront in September 1977, designed not only to cater for conferences, but for sporting events and concerts too.

Q38: A. IT WAS STOLEN

There is now a street, 'Ovett Gardens,' named after him in Gateshead.

Q39: B. EDWARD WELD

Her second husband was Thomas Fitzherbert, but he died from a chill within three years of marriage.

Q40: C. MAGNUS VOLK

He also invented the electric railway – the very first in the world – which still runs east of the Palace Pier towards Black Rock.

It is the fashion to run down George IV, but what myriads of Londoners ought to thank him for inventing Brighton! One of the best physicians our city has ever known, is kind, cheerful, merry Doctor Brighton.

W. M. THACKERAY, *THE NEWCOMES*

WORK AND PLAY

Q41: A. THE BRONZE AGE

It was found along with a bronze dagger and a stone axe, suggesting that this was a society in which some families and individuals had grown to be very important.

Q42: D. A GLASS VASE

The villa seems to have been built in two stages; it had geometric black and white mosaic floors, and in its grounds there were wells lined with chalk blocks.

Q43: A. HALL

Portslade only had two villagers and was worth only 12 shillings (just 60p)!

Q44: D. LITTLE ALLEYWAYS

The Lanes are commonly taken to be bounded by North Street to the north, Ship Street to the west and Prince Albert Street and the north side of Bartholomew Square to the south. The eastern boundary is less well-defined and can be considered either East Street or Market Street.

Q45: A. A BRIGHTON HOGGIE

With their fleet of trusty hoggies, the jugs (fishermen) not only fished off the Sussex coast, but caught mackerel and herring in the English Channel and sailed as far as the North Sea.

Q46: D. YELLOW TEETH

Dr Russell also sold pills made from crabs' eyes, woodlice, snails, vipers' flesh and tar!

Q47: C. STABLES AND RIDING SCHOOL

George disliked being watched by the public and the underground passage was his solution.

Q48: A. IRON

The mahogany handrails are carved with nodes to make them look like bamboo.

Q49: C. 3

Not everyone admired the Royal Pavilion. The writer William Cobbett said its roofscape looked like a row of upended turnips. Another critic thought St Paul's Cathedral must have had a litter of puppies on the south coast.

Q50: B. CLAY TILES THAT LOOK LIKE BRICKS

Here's a tip for mathematical tile hunters: they have little depth, so take a close look at the 'bricks' at the corner of a building – they're quite a give-away.

Q51: A. AN ICE HOCKEY CLUB

The team existed from 1935 until 1965 and was one of the United Kingdom's most successful sides during that period.

Q52: C. LONDON BRIDGE

The record time for a London–Brighton stagecoach run (in February 1834) was 3 hours 40 minutes. Most took quite a bit longer. Express trains were soon completing the journey in 1 hour 45 minutes.

Q53: B. THE DADDY-LONG-LEGS

It was the creation of Magnus Volk, the son of a German clockmaker who was born in Brighton in 1851. In 1888, he built an electric car.

Q54: B. ORGAN RECITALS

Eugenius Birch, the architect who designed the Aquarium in 1872, also designed the West Pier in 1866.

Q55: A. IT WAS TOO NOISY

The clock has four seated female statues on its red granite base, while above are four mosaic portraits, including one of Queen Victoria.

Q56: B. THE TORSO OF A YOUNG WOMAN

The legs were found in a suitcase at King's Cross Station in London.

Q57: A. A BOMB WAS DROPPED

Two adults, a teenager and a six-year-old girl were killed outright. Many others were wounded, and six more children and four adults later died of their injuries in hospital.

Q58: B. 52

It was the very first of a new crop of 'red-brick' universities throughout Britain. Sir Basil Spence designed the first buildings.

Q59: C. KIPPERS WERE TAKEN OFF THE MENU

This luxury Pullman train used to run three times a day between London and the coast, but eventually it became too expensive to run and British Rail withdrew the service.

Q60: A. *QUADROPHENIA*

The riots were between Mods (who wore smart clothes and rode about on motor scooters) and Rockers (who looked tough, wore leathers and rode motorbikes).

Q61: C. A MEDIEVAL FIELD

This is now an exciting, offbeat area packed with wacky one-off shops.

Q62: A. FALMER

The pond is still at Falmer, yellow or not, more than a thousand years later.

Q63: B. BRIGHTON SEA WATER

Drinking and swimming in Brighton sea water supposedly got rid of tumours and 'eruptions', cleared your head and kept your bowels regular.

Q64: C. CHARLES LAMB

If you wanted to take the plunge into the sea at Brighton (dressed in a long, shapeless gown), the accepted thing to do was to pay a 'dipper' to look after you.

Q65: A. AN INDIAN TAKEAWAY

It was opened by Sake Dean Mahomed and it failed. He was also the first Indian to write a book in the English language, *The Travels of Dean Mahomed*.

Q66: B. TO FOLLOW HER SWEETHEART

In old age, she sold small items, such as oranges and gingerbread, on a street corner near the Brighton Pavilion. She became a celebrity in Brighton, due to her great age and unusual experiences.

Q67: C. SUSSEX SQUARE

The Grade I listed houses of Sussex Square – a listing on a par with the finest historic buildings in the UK – were built by Thomas Read Kemp 190 years ago.

Q68: D. THE WHITE LADY

In the garden of Preston Manor there is a pets' cemetery. Here you'll find the graves of a Town Hall Cat, a Pavilion cat and poor Sooty, 'who was cruelly poisoined'.

Q69: D. 774

Although there are other strong contenders, The Cricketers claims to be the oldest pub in Brighton, supposedly opening for the first time back in 1547.

Q70: D. ST PAUL

It was built for the Reverend Arthur Wagner on West Street and became a principal church of the Tractarian movement.

Q71: D. *HARD TIMES*

Some other novels that have parts set in Brighton include *Pride and Prejudice*, *Dombey and Son*, *The Newcomes*, *Ovingdean Grange*, *New Grub Street*, *Hilda Lessways* and *Hangover Square*.

Q72: B. ROTTINGDEAN

In the Domesday Book Rottingdean was listed as having ten smallholders and being worth £3.

A VERY PECULIAR HISTORY
QUIZ BOOKS

OTHER TITLES IN THIS SERIES: